Char-cuterie from scratch

Char-cuterie from scratch

Tim Hayward

slow down, salt, dry and cure

photography by Chris Terry
illustrations by Lucia Vinti

Hardie Grant

QUADRILLE

Contents

The keys to charcuterie

What is charcuterie?

Why do we have to steal a French word for such an important part of our cuisine? We don't actually have an English word for *charcuterie* – in fact come to think of it, there isn't an English word for cuisine – but charcuterie's root is in *chair*, meaning flesh and *cuit* meaning cooked. A *charcutier* prepares and sells cooked and cured meats, particularly pork.

Charcuterie happens all over the world and is fundamentally about **preserving**. In cultures where the pig is eaten, it's about slaughtering the animal at the end of autumn, when it's fattest and before it starts to consume its own stocks of fat, and then preparing as much of the meat as possible to carry the family through the winter. For the millennia before refrigeration and freezing, this was done by a variety of methods, all of which have the same objective, in modern scientific terms – to make food into a hostile environment for harmful bacteria. Most of the organisms that cause decomposition require moisture, air and warmth to prosper. They will die if over-heated – i.e. cooked – or outside a quite narrow range of acidity/alkalinity.

Many of these techniques are older than history and have been passed on orally until very recently, but they are still based on this fundamental science. Farm workers and agricultural families who dealt with the initial preservation of meat were almost never literate and recipes passed by word of mouth. This is why, in the UK, for example, there are hundreds of different 'regional cures' for bacon or ham, dry and wet brines with all kinds of additional ingredients, but all of which simply raise the salinity of the meat higher than bacteria can survive.

Sea captains and naval officers, however, could often read and write well. In Cambridge University Library, where I researched this book, there are few recipes for pork salting from farms, but a vast collection of seafarers' logbooks, detailing the precise recipes by which meat was preserved for long voyages.

These days we have excellent refrigeration, from the point at which an animal is slaughtered, through chilled delivery trucks to fridges at the grocery store cabinets, right into the fridges in our own kitchens. We don't need to preserve food for survival, but we still do it for the amazing flavours and textures that these techniques can impart.

So why from scratch?

There's quite marvellous charcuterie to be had from your local artisan butcher, from the deli or even, at a pinch, from the grocery store, so nobody is suggesting that you cure your own bacon every autumn or make sausages once a month for the rest of your life. But just once is enough to make the connection; to understand bacon and its **history**, to appreciate salami and its **cultural significance** in a far deeper way than from the glib rubric on the back of the packet.

Across much of the world, home preserving is a way of life. Hunting doesn't have the same aristocratic connotations as it has in the UK and is enjoyed by all sorts of people. In the USA and Europe recreational hunters are used to butchering their kill, smoking, drying or otherwise preserving it, often in a suburban garage with equipment bought from a local hardware store. While in the UK, air-drying a ham might be considered either an obscure hobby or something left to specialists, in Italy or Tennessee you're just as likely to find one hanging in the garden shed as a bike or a lawnmower.

What's most noticeable is that in other food cultures, these exercises in preserving are not seen as the weird pursuits of a food freak, but just part of the seasonal duties of the household.

It's vital we understand the food we eat, where it's from and how it's altered before we consume it. In modern life we have to consume food that's been passed through various processes, industrial or otherwise – we need to understand those processes to make informed choices. It's empowering to understand how something works even if you choose never to put that knowledge into action.

Of course, you might get bitten. Alongside artisan bakers, microbrewers and cheesemongers, there are now nouveau charcutiers, selling through craft butchers, to restaurants and at farmers' markets all over the country, who have rediscovered these techniques and used them to change their lives. But, to begin with, at least, let's just acknowledge that, in a strange geeky way, some of these skills are a pleasure in themselves and worth trying if only once.

The art of managing decay

Most of us, at some time, will have experienced what happens to a piece of meat when it's left unattended for too long. Decay is not something that you're likely to forget. Preserving is the art of managing decay, so it's worth looking at what happens in animal flesh during slaughter and afterwards. The meat we eat is largely composed of muscle – along with some fat, connective tissue and other bits. Animal muscle operates by burning oxygen, supplied from the lungs by the circulatory system, and turning it into movement. As with any chemical reaction there are waste products, in this case **lactic acid**, which can build up in the muscles until it is carried away, also by the circulatory system, to be excreted.

If you run, or work out at a gym, you may be aware of the 'burn' that occurs in a freshly worked muscle as the lactic acid builds up and begins to attack it – provoking a feeling of irritation or pain. When an animal is slaughtered, the circulatory system immediately stops and lactic acid can no longer be flushed from the muscles. If an animal has been in a state of

muscular tension prior to death (and that can mean standing and moving rather than asleep), then the resulting, built-up lactic acid will continue to attack the muscles and connective tissue.

Take, then, a piece of well-shot game or a cleanly slaughtered cow, hang it somewhere that's not freezing, and it will, without any further intervention, begin to break down its own fibres. This process, sometimes called '**hanging**' or '**ageing**', is used in a controlled way to make meat more tender in texture and to develop flavour.

As the lactic acid begins to break down cells in the tissue, enzymes are released that also attack or consume surrounding tissue, a process called '**autolysis**'. At the same time bacteria will establish a hold on the meat, usually at the surface, followed by other organisms, from moulds and fungi to insects. As this process continues, with the meat being consumed from within and by outside agents, we begin to experience the signs we interpret as rot, festering, decay or putrefaction.

Bacteria and mould

Home-curers have a complex relationship with mould. It can be the first sign of spoilage or the vital ingredient in successful preservation. Gardeners define a weed as any plant that's growing in the wrong place, and we could probably look at moulds the same way.

Moulds are fungi and come in two forms. Some grow as multi-cellular strings, or hyphae, which gives the characteristic 'furry' appearance. Others are single-cell types, which we call yeasts – so we couldn't have bread, beer, cheese, soy sauce or any one of a million other food products without mould. That doesn't help, though, when your bacon has grown fur and you're wondering whether it's safe to eat.

Perhaps the most widely known food mould is the genus *Penicillium*, which has the ability to kill a variety of unpleasant bacteria. Species of penicillium crop up throughout the food world. The wonderfully evocative *P. nalgiovense* forms the white 'chalky' coating you'll have seen on the surface of a good salami, which not only protects it from bacterial growth but adds subtly to the development of flavour. It was from *P. chrysogenum* that Alexander Fleming extracted penicillin, the life-saving antibiotic, in 1929.

Good preservation is often a matter of understanding the relationships between the things that want to live on your food and balancing them against each other. Bacteria like *lactobacilli* turn the lactose in food into lactic acid, thereby creating a hostile **environment** for other organisms. A surface coating of penicillium mould kills other bacteria. These combinations of life-forms, tiny ecologies, if you will, are often subtly different from place to place. The flavour of hung meat varies depending on the environment of the chiller or fridge in which it's aged. In a charcuterie that's been used for the purpose for, say, 100 years, the combination of airborne wildlife is as unique as that in French cheese 'caves', and may be as worthy of careful conservation.

Excluding air

Bacteria need air to thrive, so some of the simplest methods of preservation simply prevent air from reaching the food. Sausage skins, to some extent, provide a physical barrier to air and, because they shrink as they dry, they also drive out small air pockets in the meat. Some foods cooked with sufficient fat – confits, for example – are automatically '**sealed**' when the fat congeals on cooling. Others, like potted meats, need a layer of clarified butter or lard poured over the surface to create an airtight '**cap**'. Later generations invented the tin can and the vacuum-pack pouch, but these traditional recipes use the very simplest methods to exclude the air.

Getting started

The instructions in the book can be treated as ordinary recipes but it's better if you treat them as starting points for your own experiments. I treat cooking and preparing food as an adventure, so, instead of trying to be comprehensive in the choice of starting points, I've shamelessly picked out those projects that are the most fun, the most rewarding, and which, I hope, will inspire your own adventures.

It's worth remembering though, that these processes will probably be new to you so it's important to read through the explanations of the processes before jumping forward to the recipes. It really helps give context if you know 'why' you're doing something, not just how to do it.

A note on measurements
I work in grams – including liquids. Most liquids we use in the kitchen weigh in at roughly 1ml = 1g – at least, that's good enough for the first trial of an existing recipe and better than trying to get a sensible measurement from something printed on the side of a fifty-year-old plastic jug. We've supplied imperial measurements where necessary. I have avoided giving serving sizes, as by their very nature many charcuterie recipes are 'cut and come again' – intended to be stored over time and nibbled at delightful leisure.

Methods of preservation

Methods of preservation

Bacteria cannot survive at temperatures above about 65°C (149°F) – which explains one of the reasons we cook things – but they also can't function below a moisture level of around 13%. For this reason, a food product that has been dried can have an effectively indefinite life – food has survived burial in the dry conditions of Egyptian tombs. In climates where food cannot be dried immediately by the sun or wind, salt or sugar can be used to 'suck' moisture out by osmosis. Because bacteria themselves are also subject to osmosis, they may be destroyed by the concentrated sugar or salt.

Cooking food halts the process of self-consumption but, once it has cooled, it is still open to bacterial attack, so methods of sealing the surface – with oil, syrup, fat or an impermeable membrane like sausage skin – physically block access.

Strongly acidic environments are lethal to bacteria, so **pickling** in vinegar or citrus can preserve some food well. Acidic solutions are also used as a topical treatment for undesirable moulds during, for example, **drying** and **salting**.

Smoking, the final method of preservation, creates an atmospheric environment hostile to organisms – nothing wants to fly through acrid smoke to lay its eggs on a ham – which enables the process of gentle air-drying to take place. In other cases, it actually deposits a layer on the surface of the food which is toxic to bacteria.

Our various methods of preservation have been evolving almost as long as man has been eating, so many recipes and techniques combine elements of more than one process – a ham can be aged, salted, air-dried, smoked and eventually wrapped airtight and frozen. Understanding all of them is man's way of conquering decay.

Curing & salting

People have been salting since ancient Egypt. The technique of powdering flesh with salt and '**natron**' (that's saltpetre) and burying it in sand to dry out worked just as well for hams as it did for the bodies of kings. All over the world, from the beams of a Tennessee cabin to the lofts of Parma, salt pork hangs drying. It's not some high-tech mystery; any person with access to a pig and salt has made bacon. Hell, my nan salted pork in a council house.

Bacon used to be home-cured in sides or '**flitches**', which, I have to admit, is a tempting thought, if a little unwieldy for the domestic setting. William Cobbett, in *Cottage Economy* (1821), reckoned that owning a flitch or two did wonderful things to the morals of the peasantry: 'The sight of them upon the rack tends more to keep a man from stealing than whole volumes of penal statutes.'

A domestic pig would live in close symbiosis with its owner, foraging for its own food, as well as neatly hoovering up any waste the family produced. After a year of fattening, the pig was slaughtered and every bit, from bristles to blood, was used in some productive way. Without refrigeration, though, preservation was vital. Pigs were usually slaughtered at the beginning of the winter, when cold weather kept the meat fresh during processing, but mainly so that there would be a stock of salted products to carry the family through the tough months of annual famine.

The most common method of salting was to pack pieces of pork in a barrel of dry salt. **Osmosis** drew liquid from the meat, which leached out of the bottom of the barrel, creating an environment in which bacteria couldn't survive. This kind of rough salted pork was the winter staple wherever pigs were kept. It was also a vital part of the rations aboard ships and for armies on the move.

It wouldn't suit our modern palates. Much like salt fish, it would have benefited from a long soaking in 'many waters' to wash out enough salt to make it edible. This strong saltiness was probably the reason people experimented with sweeter cures once refined sugar and molasses became available and, eventually, inexpensive. They have a similar preservative effect to salt but can balance the saltiness on the palate. Most modern cures combine salt and sugar in varying proportions, depending on taste.

Bacon

Let's start, as all the best days should, with bacon. According to *The Grocer*, a magazine that specializes in such arcana, the average Brit eats bacon three times a week – a rise in sales due to the growing popularity of 'premium and organic bacon'. That's marvellous news both for the producers and for those discerning souls who still reckon that a piece of bacon should sizzle when it hits a hot pan, not yield a great puddle of milky fluid and a vague smell of fish.

The average American eats around 18lb of bacon per year. A fabulous statistic when you realize that, if that's an average, then for every vegetarian, vegan, Muslim, Jew or even 'person who's not crazy about bacon' in the US, there's somebody who's consuming 36lb of bacon per year.

We do, however, pay dearly for our discernment. Fashionably artisanal bacon from organic pigs can cost about twice the price of the pork it's made from. That's an impressive mark-up for one of the oldest and simplest processes of meat preservation.

What is that white liquid?

Many years ago, butchers discovered that a syringe-like device could be used to inject pork with **brine**. This made the curing process quicker and ensured that all the meat was properly salted right through. Butchers, of course, are not without guile, and it didn't take long for them to work out that, while dry-cured bacon loses weight as it cures,[1] injection curing could actually increase the weight of the meat and thus profit.

When we think we're paying for bacon in a grocery store, we're all too often buying water – well, not exactly 'buying', more 'renting', because the minute that juicy rasher (bacon slice) hits your frying pan it dumps its load in that dispiriting pool of milky white liquid in which it proceeds to poach into a disappointing, leathery scrap.

Your own bacon won't yield any water in the pan, an experience you may initially find disorientating. Please be brave though, keep your eyes on the prize and plough through. If bacon was meant to have that much salty water in it, pigs would have evolved gills.

---

[1] *Pigs for Breeders and Feeders*, by Sanders Spencer, with a chapter on bacon curing by Loudon M. Douglas (London: Vinton [1908]), ends with the following warning: 'It must be borne in mind that the longer either bacon or hams hang in the smokehouse the greater will be the loss of weight.'

Nitrites

The main noticeable difference between traditional salt pork and modern bacon is the colour. Cured pork is an unappetizing grey and cooks up to a thrilling beige. Modern bacon owes its healthy pink to **sodium nitrite**.

In commercial curing, nitrites are added to maintain the colour and, more importantly, as a kind of total insurance against botulism in an industrial production environment. Some scientists believe they have established links between heavy consumption of nitrites over long periods and some forms of cancer, but not to such an extent that governments have done anything more than give recommended maximum dosages.

Some home-curers work entirely without nitrites – in fact, many give the avoidance of nitrite additives as the main reason they cure. I'm a nitrite fan. Removing the tiny risk of botulism is a reassuring benefit, and grey bacon is harder to sell to children and dinner guests. But this is an entirely personal choice.

Drying

We used to have a fantastic tradition of salting meat in the UK, though not perhaps with the self-publicizing elan of other nations (York, Wiltshire and Bradenham have been names associated with various hams, and our bacon was ever legendary, but they were never really star players on the international platter of cold meats), but, perhaps because we like our bangers fresh and our bacon salty, we've never quite got round to drying stuff.

It's a shame really, because everyone else has got something hanging out the back: bresaola, jerky, droëwors, Bündnerfleisch, biltong, salami, kabanosy, lap cheong, chorizo, saucisson sec and innumerable others. There's a common belief that we don't 'do charcuterie' in the UK because our humid climate makes meat 'go off' rather than dry; that's a complete myth. You actually need a **cool, moist environment** for curing, preferably with a decent breeze. If a sausage or piece of meat dries quickly in dry air the outside becomes hard too quickly – '**case hardened**' – preventing the moisture from escaping from the centre. In moist air the outer surface remains pliable as the meat dries evenly throughout. Most of the best charcuterie in the world is cured in moist temperate climates, often in mountains or where a good clean sea-breeze can promote drying through **evaporation**.

This is obviously not an accurate description of conditions in my backyard, but I've had great success drying meat in my kitchen, hanging it close to a north-facing window for maximum chill and breeze through the tired sashes. I also tend to hang it over the sink to keep the humidity up. If things get too hot I move it to the shade. In fact, the more you can keep an eye on your meat, checking it daily, the better result you're likely to get.

People often ask 'What do you mean by "cool"?'. One look at the way I dress should tell you I'm the wrong bloke to ask, but where charcuterie is concerned, the answer is mercifully easier. Meat needs to be hung at a temperature high enough that fermentation can take place, but low enough to discourage bacteria and molds. The magic window is 10–15°C or 50–60°F. If only it was that easy to make a decision about how to wear your baseball cap.

Many home-curers starting out get jumpy when mould appears. Actually, a chalk-white bloom on the surface is healthy, and any spots of slimy or black mould can be quickly removed with plain vinegar – another good reason for a daily check. The best reassurance, though, is a good deep sniff. If your meat is going off you'll definitely know by the smell – in fact, in Italy this is still considered the only sure way to check. Testers use a long needle made from horse bone, which can be slid into the ham or salami and sniffed to ensure there's no trace of putrescence.

I've been forced to the conclusion that, love as we do our hams, bangers, bacons and chops, we Brits are funny about pork. Nominally sane people who'll happily wolf street food in the most 'authentic' of milieus, who harbour an ambition to try fugu and will cheerfully eat takeaway sushi from a convenience store, will blanch, gag and retch if served pork properly pink near the bone.

They'll reel off a litany of ill-informed nonsense about trichinosis, some vague superstition about how it 'tastes a bit like human flesh' and then go off into a load of ranting cobblers about worms. Then you offer them a bit of home-cured salami and they go right off the rails. Come on. That half of the population of the world who don't reject pork out of hand have been salting and air-drying pork for as long as they've domesticated the pig. What can be the problem?

Once chopped meat has been salted and packed in a robust natural skin, it's proof against most that the elements can throw at it and creates an environment hostile to bacteria. Once that's sorted, time and the free flow of air will dry it out, making any kind of spoilage even more unlikely. That, as they say, is the science bit. So simple that millions of illiterate peasants have been doing it, all over the world, every year for countless centuries, feeding it to their beloved and treasured families throughout the winter and not just surviving but apparently enjoying the results.

Some of the most highly refined connoisseur snobbery in the food world is reserved for air-dried pork in the form of *jamón ibérico* or *prosciutto di Parma*, and it is true that curing and air-drying a whole leg is technically challenging. Maintaining conditions under which the curing salt can penetrate the dense muscular flesh of a whole ham is not something you can easily achieve in the average garden shed, but thinner cuts – belly for pancetta, for example – or roughly chopped meat allow the salt to penetrate more surely.

After the first couple of tries, pride and greed overcome any lurking superstitious worries or general mimsy gutlessness.

> 'You mean you chop up a load of pork, stuff it in a pig gut and
>   hang it outside for a month… in England?'
> Damn right I do… and so should you.

More good things

When I visited charcuteries on early trips to France I loved the sausages, of course, the mountain hams and potent local artisanal salamis, but I was mortified to see something that looked like luncheon meat baked into a bun.

> 'What is it?' I enquired in my hopeless French.
> '*Ça, monsieur, c'est un saucisson brioché.*'

My eyes would have rolled into the back of my head at this shameless appropriation of the Great British sausage roll had they not suddenly lit, in a combination of horror and outraged *amour propre*, on something labelled '**Pâté en croute**'… a square section of preserved meat and pastry that was, in all but name, a pork pie. It dawned on me then that the greatest triumphs of the charcutier's art had direct equivalents on my side of the Channel too.

There was a time when every British high street had two butchers. There was the regular butcher, in whose window you'd see great sides of beef, whole lambs, poultry and game and then, a little bit further along the street was the pork butcher, from whom you could obtain a pork chop, if such was your fancy, but mainly where you went for sausages, bacon and a vast selection of cooked and preserved pork products. This was nothing to do with snobbery or even some hangover from control by trade guilds; the butcher was set up to buy in large pieces of red meat and reduce them to '**joints**' and pieces to be cooked at home, while the pork butcher often reared and slaughtered his own pigs but was equipped to salt, to pickle, and most importantly, to cook.

The pork butcher made brawn, haslet and hough – direct equivalents of pâtés and *tête de veau* (calf's head). Some made odd regional variations like Bath chaps[1] or Lincolnshire chine – *jambon persillé* (parsleyed ham or ham in parsley aspic) in all but name. Pretty much everywhere in the country, though, you'd expect your pork butcher to make a great pork pie.

There were, of course, by-products of all this gleeful manufacture. Pig fat was sold by the pork butcher as lard – in a nation without olive oil, lard was the most important cooking fat available. There was also plenty of trimming and waste meat, all of which was carefully hoarded and turned into sausages.

[1] the Bath chap is a brined pig cheek that's been rolled into a cone, breadcrumbed and deep fried. Don't knock it till you've tried it.

Equipment & ingredients

Equipment

Scales and weighing

I use domestic electronic scales from a department store – they are fine for measurements from around 10g to 5000g and stow in a drawer. I have a special pocket electronic scale, accurate to 0.1 of a gram, which I use for the small stuff. These are popular with baristas and drug dealers, are inexpensive and can be bought wherever bongs and incense are sold (or on the internet).

For really large pieces of meat, you might find your kitchen scale inadequate but you could try the bathroom type. Mine is capable of measuring my substantial bulk with really quite depressing accuracy, so it's more than capable of handling big animal chunks.

When I give the odd half a gram measurement here or there, I'm not necessarily expecting the reader to weigh it any more than I expect them to whip out a micrometer when I say: 'Chop carrots into 1cm/½ inch dice'. I do expect people to be able to judge and I give them the best information with which to do so.

Thermometer

I give internal temperatures because they are the only scientific way of working and, though a few years ago a probe thermometer was a piece of science-fiction kit, they are now absolute standard in the catering industry and can be bought easily and cheaply from a catering supplier.[1]

[1] You can buy a digital probe thermometer from most kitchen supply companies. All are a lot more accurate than traditional thermometers and will revolutionize your cooking. Do be aware, though, that having to wait for every reading can become wearing after a while, so go for the 'instant read' type. I favour the Thermapen (see Suppliers on page 142), which is instant and can handle fats and boiling sugar syrups. The only downside is that pulling out the neatly folded probe – which automatically switches it on and off – can be a bit fiddly. I live in permanent hope that they'll develop some sort of sprung 'flick-knife' version which will revolutionize chefs' lives.

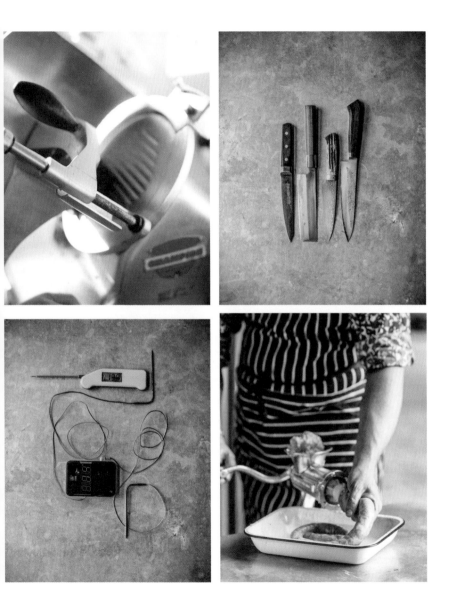

By law, food served to the public has to have its internal temperature checked and recorded, which means that the pub barman and the dinner lady at school all use probe thermometers, routinely taking and judging internal food temperatures. If they can do it, we can, and our home cooking and the results of our recipes will improve immeasurably.

Proper, accurate measuring kit is now cheap and widely available. You don't have to buy a Thermapen and an electronic scale, but I think, if we're going to take the business of cooking seriously enough to buy cupcake machines, breadmakers, water filters and juicers, we should probably bite the bullet and get the measuring tools up to speed first. I wouldn't suggest you took up carpentry without a ruler and a square, because without correct lengths and angles it fails. Cooking is all about quantities, times and temperatures – we can no more work without accurate scales and thermometers than we could without a clock or watch.

Vacuum-packer

The vacuum-packer is the charcutier's secret weapon. About the size and shape of a small printer, it sucks all the air out of a special plastic food bag and then welds it closed and airtight. Curing and maturing products in the fridge can be a smelly business, but vacuum-packing means you can share space without cross-contamination.

Some gadgets can seem pointless, but a vacuum-packer replaces a small suite of carefully ventilated curing rooms, hanging cellars, a salting trough and half a dozen other things that no longer exist in the average non-stately home. It constitutes a pretty serious tool investment, but look at it this way: once you can professionally pack homemade salami and bacon to give as gifts to grateful family, it'll pay for itself in the first Christmas.

All sorts of meat can be dry-cured in a vacuum-pack and the **anaerobic** environment adds an extra level of security against bacteria. Curing sides can be stacked in the fridge and turned daily to ensure even penetration of salt.

Hand-operated mincer

It's possible to buy hand-operated mincers (meat grinders) which not only chop the meat but also, with the blade removed, pack it into the skin for you. These are reasonably successful, but producing a single kilo of sausage will leave you with a hypertrophic forearm like a fiddler crab on steroids. Far better to search the houses of friends and relatives and seek out the individual with the biggest kitchen mixer. The best can be fitted with a mincer, so it's worth clubbing together with friends to buy the attachment for the rare occasions it will be used.

Knives and slicers

You won't need any extra knives and slicers for charcuterie, as long as you have something with which you're comfortable chopping raw meat and something for slicing the finished result.

For chopping, you need something with a good broad heavy blade and a wickedly sharp edge. I personally favour a lightweight Chinese cleaver (*cai dao*) but a standard chef knife would be the more traditional choice. To get even finer dice when hand chopping, it's worth putting the meat (and particularly any fat) into the freezer until it begins to stiffen up a little. Not totally frozen but just solidified enough to make it easier to handle.

I found my vintage 1930s slicer in a junk shop. It still does a good job but contravenes pretty much every health and safety regulation there is. Safer, smaller and perhaps more practical electric slicers are available from commercial kitchen supply houses. They're not cheap, so see if you can find one second hand.

The sausage horn

A sausage horn or nozzle is not vital but it makes shovelling mince into a damp piece of casing a minor chore rather than an extended comedy sketch. If you own a mincer (meat grinder) you may find that a set of horns – in various sizes to fit the bore of the different casings – comes as an accessory. If you can find these, remove the blade from your mincer and attach the nozzle, loaded with casings, then the mincer's helical drive will act as a packing machine, forcing the meat into the sausages.

If you don't have a mincer, a set of plastic horns won't cost much and you can pack the meat in with a combination of spoon and vigorous application of the thumb.

Always try to avoid air bubbles when packing the skins; they can cause a banger to burst and are occasionally hideaways for spoilage bacteria.

Building a hanging cage

During colder months, if there's no rain or frost, it's great to dry outdoors. Cold winds speed up evaporation while the generally moister air stops the outer surface of the meat from becoming hard and impermeable, so the meat dries at an equal speed throughout. Both Parma and Appalachian 'country' ham rely on the cold/moist/windy climate combination and that's some of the finest ham in the world. It's possible to do it in the UK, or more unsettled climates, but you'll need to keep a close eye on the weather and to keep inquisitive animals off the project.

A hanging cage looks not unlike a giant bird feeder. I've made one from two sheets of 1cm/½ inch steel mesh, laid on top of each other at a 0.5cm/¼ inch offset and stitched into a tube with galvanized wire. I used two discs, snipped from the same material, as a floor and a lid stolen from a small-sized galvanized dustbin. The hanging frame inside is made from a couple of pieces of scrap timber and some stainless steel cup hooks. I usually dry salami or bresaola indoors for the first few days, by which point it's stopped dripping and is beginning to tighten up enough to be of less interest to bugs.

These days I hang it in the garden, where I can see it from the kitchen window, but I've lent it to friends who've used it inside a garage. Wherever you site it, it needs to be out of direct sunlight, with a clear flow of air around and through it and high enough that it won't be troubled by animals. Squirrels and birds are welcome to have a go, but they can't reach far enough through the bars and the lid ensures they can't climb up above it.

I've never had a problem with flies, as I usually find elements like vinegar and pepper in the marinades keep them off, but it might well be possible to build the whole project in perforated zinc which is also flyproof.

In the past, I've left meat in my hanging cage through light rain and very heavy snow without losing so much as a sausage, but if at any point you're worried, just keep it inside, somewhere cool, until the weather improves.

Building a jerky box

Jerky and biltong both require **dry heat**. There are commercial desiccators for the process, and people with an AGA (range) often swear by the bottom oven, but a jerky box is easy to build and allows much more control.

The heat source is one of those incandescent light bulbs. They're not terribly green because of the enormous amount of energy they put out as heat rather than light – though in this case it works to our advantage. This might be the only remaining ethical use for such out-of-date technology.

Because not much heat is involved, the enclosure can be as simple as a cardboard box or something more elaborate in wood (see opposite) or metal if you feel like going into mass production – however you tackle it, though, the principles are the same. You're just creating a chimney so that the hot dry air can flow up and over the hanging meat.

You can use the box for jerky, biltong or droëwors, but remember that things like bresaola, ham, salami, etc. need a longer, more gentle process to retain their texture, so don't be tempted to hurry them along in your box.

Building a dry-curing box

If you can, persuade your local wine shop to give you one of those flattish wooden crates, the sort that store wine bottles on their sides – a lid is nice but not essential – and rig up some way of catching the liquid in a bucket or bowl. Mix up your cure in a big enough quantity to create a thick layer on the bottom of the box, then lay in your pork piece and heap more cure over the top. A dry-curing box like this is closest to the original farmhouse method. Any liquid from the meat drips through the bottom of the box and it's easy to check the state of the cure regularly.

Perhaps a more modern approach is to buy two of those large plastic boxes that are good for storage. Stack them one inside the other, then drill holes in the bottom of the top box. This will now remain clear of the liquid as long as you remember to empty the bottom box regularly.

Ingredients

Buying meat

We all want to use good-quality meat from sustainable sources with high-welfare standards and you will already have good sources for this, but charcuterie often requires different **cuts**, with different qualities to those you might be used to looking for. You might require fatty meat, strongly flavoured, almost gamey pork or a single, complete muscle.

The best piece of advice I can give, in charcuterie… in all cooking and quite possibly, in life, is to build a good relationship with your butcher. Even if your regular butcher doesn't do a lot of curing in the store, he or she will have learned a lot about it during their training and apprenticeship. They seem happy to help, indeed even enthusiastic, and you'll soon find yourself picking up all kinds of hints and tips.

Salt

You will find yourself using a quite ridiculous amount of salt while curing and if you apply the usual rule, of buying the high-quality flaky stuff, you will undoubtedly end your days in debtor's prison. On the other hand, you don't want to be curing with the regular grocery store salt, which is combined with 'anti-caking agents'. These can concentrate in the cured meat and give unpleasant aftertastes. Definitely don't use the stuff designed for dishwashers or indeed, as a tight-fisted mate of mine once did, try to salt hams in the salt they sell for de-icing paths.

Coarse grain sea salt is usually quite cheap and unadulterated. I have also discovered that health food stores often stock big bags of a sort of damp, grey sea salt which is intended for people of a particular quirk of mind to use in their bath. It is entirely pure and cheap in quantity, though do check the packet before using, to ensure it doesn't contain anything other than salt.

A note on herbs

Traditionally, recipes have given two different quantities for herbs: one for the nice fresh stuff, another for the dried-up old dust that's been in the back of the cupboard since 1978. Today, grocery stores have revolutionized the supply chain for herbs, so something like thyme will be available alive in a pot, in a cut bunch, freeze-dried, as a paste with oil or from the freezer cabinet. With the woody/oily herbs (thyme, rosemary, sage, juniper) I find that all forms (except the '78 vintage dust) work equally well. These are the quantities I've given but, as with all flavourings, the amounts are guidelines only – perhaps the single most important kitchen technique to develop is constant **tasting**.

Sausages

Sausages require little more than pork, seasonings, casings and a mincer (meat grinder) – see Equipment on page 35.

Sausage skins (casings)

Sausage skins, or 'casings' as they're known in the butchery trade, are traditionally made from cleaned lengths of the digestive tract. There are obviously some fairly stringent methods employed to clean what is effectively a pipe full of poop.

Lengths of gut are turned inside out, scraped to remove the soft lining material and repeatedly washed. What's left is a tough membrane, impermeable to liquids; edible, though without any flavour; that shrinks as it dries.

You can order casings from your butcher or any of the online suppliers in the list on page 142. They will arrive salted, vacuum-packed and probably in ludicrous lengths. Trust me, there are few more satisfying sounds than that of 40 metres/130 feet of pig gut landing on your doorstep. First thing to do is unpack and sort them. Cut them into manageable lengths of about a metre/3 feet, and then repack them into smaller batches and freeze. They'll keep indefinitely in the freezer.

To use a batch of natural casings, unpack them and soak in several changes of clean water. This will remove the salt and make them softer and more manageable. There's no polite way of describing the next bit. You need to pick up the wet membrane and slide it on to your sausage horn like a wet sock, wrinkling it up so you can pack as much on as possible. You'll probably be able to load it up with several metre lengths.

Different gauges of sausage casing come from different parts of the digestive tract and from different animals. Medium to large size, from the large intestine of a cow or pig, will work well for fat bangers and salamis, chipolatas will need the small intestine of a pig, and merguez is usually done halal-style, using the small intestine of a lamb.

A haggis, monstrous boiled delight that it is, uses 'ox-bung', probably the least euphemistic euphemism ever for the very last metre or so of the cow's alimentary canal.

Pig's blood
Your butcher may be able to supply pig's blood if you ask nicely and well in advance. Traders dealing with pork at farmers' markets are always a good bet too. They usually have some sort of relationship with the abattoir and may well be sympathetic to your experiments.

In order to prevent clotting, the blood should have a little vinegar added and preferably be stirred regularly. If you can't get your hands on fresh blood, you should be able to buy the pasteurized and dried variety from a butcher's supply house. There's no shame in this. Food hygiene regulations mean that many artisanal manufacturers are now using the dried product.

Core recipes

Curing & salting

Basic dry cure (page 70)

The dry cure uses salt in high concentrations to draw the liquid out of the meat, and aggressive salting creates a surface environment in which no bugs can flourish. The meat is set up in such a way that the liquid flows away and the joint (roast) remains dry. In circumstances where the meat is likely to 'go off' quickly, the dry cure gets it stable much faster, though it leaves little time for any subtle flavourings to penetrate. A period of dry salting is often the prelude to more complex curing processes.

Cure flavourings

Many of the strong-flavoured 'oily' herbs – rosemary, thyme, juniper and sage in particular – are considered, even today, to have antiseptic properties. This is probably why they appear so commonly in traditional cures. In Europe, garlic is a more common addition and, as spices became more readily available, they also began to appear, particularly in dry cures.

Most of the cure recipes in this book are intentionally simple, usually with a single flavouring element. This is the best way to conduct a first experiment, a clear starting point from which to develop your own variations over time.

Basic wet cure (page 72)

In wet-curing, the brining ingredients are dissolved in water and the meat is fully immersed. Butchers used to favour this method, as it required less attention than dry-curing and possibly led to less weight loss in the meat through dehydration. If you want to wet-brine, a single plastic storage bin is a good choice of container. Pick something into which your meat can fit easily, without touching the sides, but don't overdo the size – it has to be filled deep enough with liquid to completely submerge the meat, and that can get expensive.

'It is desirable to maintain the brines in the cisterns at a uniform strength for pickling purposes and in order to determine this strength a **salinometer** is used. A jugful of the brine is taken out, and the salinometer floated in it. The strength of the brine is at once indicated on the scale, and this should never be allowed to exceed 90°C or 95°C (194°F or 203°F).'[1]

The easy cure (page 74)

The most efficient and least fussy method of modern home-curing comes halfway between wet-curing and dry-curing, using ingredients and equipment you probably already have. It's basically a dry mix of salt and sugar, rubbed into the meat and then sealed into a zip-seal freezer bag, so the 'packages' of curing meat can be stacked in the fridge and allowed to do their work with minimal intervention. As moisture leaches out of the meat, it dissolves the dry-cure ingredients, so for half the curing time it's being wet-brined.

[1] Sanders Spencer, *Pigs for Breeders and Feeders*.

Salt beef and pastrami (page 80–84)

Both salt beef and pastrami are made from brisket, a fatty, flavourful and cheap cut from the front/underside of the cow. Brisket usually comes boned and rolled and should be cured in a wet brine.

For salt beef, leave the brisket tied into a roll; if brining for pastrami, untie the piece and trim it to a neat, flat slab.

Duck 'ham' (page 88)

Farmed duck breasts are easily available in grocery stores. The meat is full of flavour and the thick fat layer is wonderfully tasty when cured. It's a smaller piece of meat, so salt quickly extracts the first moisture and hanging and drying completes the process in just a few days. Duck is also a great starting place for air-drying experiments because it tastes equally good when dried to a tight, hammy texture at 30% moisture loss or when taken on to a more leathery 'jerky' style.

If you'd like to experiment with flavourings, choose aromatic compounds that are oil-based. Thyme, rosemary and juniper are useful herbs, and dried orange peel can add a twang.

Beef

If you want to know about delis, ask a New Yorker. They'll get all misty-eyed and talk about the glory days of Katz's and the Carnegie. The first delis in Manhattan began as simple cookshops, serving kosher food to young immigrant men living away from their supportive families. As urban Jewish communities grew, they became secular cultural centres and even as later generations moved their homes from the inner city to more prosperous suburbs, the deli still served the traditionally Jewish workplaces, rag trade, diamond-dealing or theatre districts. Deli food was too good, too cheap and filling to remain a secret and it wasn't long before the giant delis so dear to the memory of New Yorkers began serving a wider audience, varying the menu to suit.

Today the New York delis that survive are a shadow of their former selves. The trade-specific districts that lent them relevance are dispersing. Their traditional customers are ageing, watching their diets or retiring to the 'burbs, so the delis have become tourist attractions where out-of towners come to marvel at the stupendous proportions of the sandwiches. The prognosis is not good.

London, which has had a settled Jewish community for much longer than Manhattan, used to boast hundreds of salt beef bars. Once they seemed a fixture on every other street corner, yet today there are around half a dozen. I write as nothing more than a greedy Gentile, but it seems to me that the demise of salt beef, though originating in Ashkenazi cuisine and firmly rooted in urban Jewish tradition, is going to be a tremendous loss to all of us; it's part of a wider picture of city eating. I regard the preservation and evangelism of proper salt beef as a duty as well as an honour.

Lardo (page 76)

Health fiends like their slices lean, but a real aficionado knows that all the **flavour is in the fat**. If that's true, then *lardo di Colonnata* must be the acme of baconly delight. This Italian *salume* is pure backfat, at least 3cm/1¼ inches thick, cured with salt and herbs. Colonnata is a district of Carrara, where the beautiful white marble of which much of Rome is built was quarried. Traditionally the lardo is cured in tanks made of Carrara marble. The sight of a slab of pure backfat, nestling in a tub of blinding white marble, might well have greeted Michelangelo when he nipped into the quarry for a lump to carve his David. Somehow, I find that thought immensely pleasurable.

If you are lucky enough to spot a piece of pork at your butcher's with a serious, unbroken fat layer, seize upon it like a dropped bank note. Although proper lardo di Colonnata is made from specially bred pigs, those occasional finds of pieces more than a couple of centimetres thick can be quickly turned into something just as glorious.

Guanciale (page 77)

Perhaps Italy's most exciting contribution to the world of bacon is *guanciale*, cured and air-dried pig cheek. Guanciale is as simple as bacon to cure but, among bacon aficionados – of whom there are a worryingly large number – it's regarded as a kind of piggy holy grail. Once you've tried pasta amatriciana with your own, home-cured guanciale, there's no going back.

Bacon cuts

I have a beautiful old brochure from the British Bacon Council pinned up over my desk. It's dated around 1960 and shows the range of cuts from a whole salted side of pig.

Names of meat cuts are notoriously confusing – there are regional and national variations, and today even many butchers won't remember the old terms, but it's worth working our way round a side just to see how things used to be. Below is my patent **PigMap™**, used to generally help out in choosing pork, no matter what obscure names the butcher might use. Take it with you into the store and point.

A good fat pig is conveniently rectangular in shape. Looking at the whole side, in general the front end and underside – the cheaper cuts – will be cured hard and called 'bacon'; the rear end and top side – more premium cuts – will be 'gammon', with a more refined, lighter cure and a shorter shelf life – better for roasting and boiling. These latter are literally 'high on the hog'.

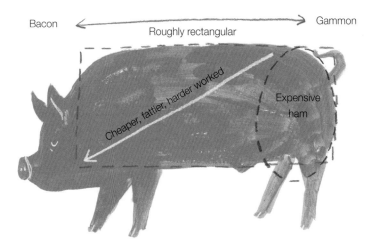

Smoking bacon

For many of us, proper bacon is smoked. After curing, leave the bacon piece uncovered in the fridge overnight. This allows the meat to dry out a little and develop a sticky coating.

Hang up your bacon in the smoker or lay it on racks and smoke to taste. I like to give both belly and back bacon a good 8 hours in the smoke, which develops a strong flavour, but many people prefer shorter times for a more subtle effect.

Whatever time you smoke it for, the bacon will benefit from 'resting' for a couple of days wrapped and in the fridge. This enables the smoky flavours deposited on the surface to equalize throughout the meat.

The natural home for smoked bacon is the bacon sandwich, or, at a pinch, the BLT, but a small quantity goes a long way in a salad. 'Lardons' (small chunks of bacon) work particularly well with bitter salad leaves like endive, escarole, frisée or, better still, dandelion, as you need something robust to take the fat. The traditional French technique would be to '**deglaze**' the pan in which the bacon had fried with a splash of wine vinegar, and use the resultant liquid as the base of a dressing. You can also make up a simple vinaigrette – heavy on the mustard – and use the leftover bacon fat to fry up a few stale bread croûtons. Well, we wouldn't want to see it go to waste, would we?

Drying

Bresaola (page 92)

Call it *bresaola*, call it spiced, air-dried beef, but it's one of the simplest bits of charcuterie to do at home. Bresaola is salted and dried just like a salami but it's made from a single muscle of beef. This means that, though the surface might develop a healthy bloom of mould while it dries, the inside of the meat is never exposed to the air, making any kind of unhelpful bacterial development much less likely. This kind of single-muscle charcuterie is the easiest to carry off successfully, so it makes a great first project if you're just dipping your toe in the water.

Salami (page 96)

The only thing vaguely disturbing about making salami at home is how easy it is, and the result is an entirely different animal to the dried-out and leathery staple of the grocery store deli. The texture is softer, fudgier, the flavours clearer, the fat and meat taste cleaner, with none of the rancid edge of long-stored 'products'. In fact the only downside I can find in staring at a length of home-cured salami is knowing I probably won't be able to stop until I've finished it.

Note that with salami we're departing from the territory of single-muscle curing and working with minced and chopped meats, which have a much larger surface area and are, therefore, an easier target for bacteria. When making salami for air-drying I'm even more careful than usual about cleanliness in the kitchen, and I don't recommend trying the recipe without using the Prague Powder (see the note on page 70).

Jerky and biltong (pages 99 and 100)

In both South Africa and parts of the USA there's a strong tradition of rapid drying of meat. Both pioneer cultures were reliant on hunting, which meant a large-sized kill often had to be preserved quickly. Lean meat was cut into thin strips and dried on gratings over a low fire, or perhaps hung in direct sunlight to drive off all moisture. Here, though, the difference ends. If you ever want to start a large punch-up, walk into any bar full of backpackers and assert that jerky and biltong are the same thing. Both cultures swear that theirs is the best and the alternative nothing better than meaty shoe leather.

Try making biltong with venison or ostrich meat, if you can get it. The important thing to remember is that the meat should be a lean single muscle. That way it remains impervious to bacteria until it's cut.

The vinegar has a very important role to play in killing surface bacteria on the cut meat, but, if you wish, you can experiment with other 'washes' after the vinegar has been applied. Worcestershire sauce (soy or teriyaki are good substitutes), whisky and even barbecue sauce are popular.

The simplest jerky would be prepared from beef or venison in much the same way as biltong, only without the vinegar or coriander. Modern jerky, though, is a very different thing; many recipes today contain incredibly complex mixtures of ingredients. My recipe is homage to my time living in the Deep South and throws in pretty much every cliché available. I suggest that in this case, you subtract to your own personal taste.

Lomo (Spanish cured pork loin) (page 102)

The pork loin is a lovely piece of meat. It's a clean single muscle which means that the interior, not being exposed to air, is entirely bacteria free, and only the surface needs to be treated before hanging. This makes it one of the easiest and most rewarding pieces to cure, and the Spanish in particular have made something of an art of it. There are many different types of lomo. Most don't use sugar in the cure, but I like the robust extra kick of the hot paprika so a little sweetness helps balance things out.

Weight loss – the magic percentage

Once most meat products have been effectively sterilized by salting, the drying process is a continuous one that depends on **airflow**, **temperature** and **humidity**. Left too long, meat will become dry and brittle. Not long enough and... well, you're effectively just eating old raw meat.

Getting it right is surprisingly simple. As water evaporates, the meat naturally loses weight. The optimum state of drying for most preserved products is when they have lost 30% of their weight.

Weigh your salami or ham carefully once it's been salted and is ready to hang. Write the date and starting weight on a cardboard swing tag and tie it on. Reweigh weekly at first and then daily as you get closer to your target weight. It's worth keeping a record of dates and weights on the tag so you begin to get a feel for how drying works: initially a rapid fall-off, slowing gently over time.

Once you hit the target point you can prevent further moisture loss by airtight packing. A vacuum-packer is ideal if you have access to one, but you can achieve great results with zip-seal freezer bags or a generous wrapping in plastic wrap.

Storing under refrigeration or even freezing stops fats becoming liquid or going rancid and extends potential storage time.

Air-dried ham

Air-dried ham is 'the big one' in the world of charcuterie. All the really aspirational brands, the Parmas, Pata Negras, Bayonnes and Westphalias, are made from whole legs of carefully reared pigs, salted and hung so that those busy *lactobacilli* can develop their complex flavours. There's a very good reason why a few ounces of the best air-dried stuff will set you back a small fortune: it's still unbelievably expensive to produce.

Feeding pigs on specialist diets – beechmast, acorns, chestnuts, etc. – rather than commercial pig feeds is old-fashioned, costly and labour-intensive. The skills involved in correctly curing such large pieces of meat are increasingly hard to find. Big slabs of pork can take years to dry properly and when a cure doesn't take – which in most processes is calculated at around one leg in twelve – a lot goes to waste at once.

Doing a whole leg as an air-dried ham is certainly possible for a home cook; the process is exactly the same as for the simpler, small pieces, but, like the big producer, you'll need to invest quite a lot of money up front, plus an enormous amount of time and care, and if you do absolutely everything right there's still that one-in-twelve chance of things going awry and having to junk the project.

More good things

Sausages (page 106)

There are few foods that reward a bit of care and attention quite as well as the simple banger. A poorly made grocery store sausage can be an awful thing, recycling the worst waste meats and packed with fillers, fluids and modifiers. Yet a properly made artisanal sausage from an honest butcher calls forth hymns of praise from the lucky consumer.

Perhaps sausages don't immediately spring to mind as a preserved product, but they are the stock-in-trade of the charcutier, rescuing and repurposing the tastiest, albeit challenging, **offcuts** and forming the starting point of the smoking and drying processes. What too few of us seem to realize is how little effort it can take to go one better and actually make our own sausages, controlling quality and flavours and producing something immeasurably more transcendent than the dispiriting meat pod in the Styrofoam tray on the chiller shelf.

Sausages generally need between 1.5 and 2% of salt; 4% is probably the highest you'll need to go in a homemade one. The best way to be sure is to start with the smallest amount and fry small test batches.

Blood sausage (page 132)

Blood sausage is probably one of the most challenging charcuterie projects for most people, as obtaining a bucket of blood, keeping it liquid and pouring it into skins in your kitchen is well beyond the comfort zone of a lot of cooks. That said, if you're untroubled by the fact that it's blood then homemade black pudding is one of the most rewarding things to make – for the simple reason that most of the commercial stuff is radically over-spiced and loses all its subtlety.

There are places where you can get into a three-month debate on seasonings and a stand-up fight over serving blood pudding. It's regarded as a national dish in parts of Ireland, Spain, rural France and the North of England… all places where the finer points of culinary debate can be ferociously defended. I tend towards a morcilla style but only because my friend Rachel McCormack, an expert on Catalan food, scares me so much that I follow her advice.

'Black pepper – and in Asturias a tiny bit of cinnamon. In Extremadura, cumin. In Burgos, onion and pine nuts. In a village in Andalucía, almonds and they also do one with quite a lot of chilli (but won't give me the bloody recipe). Mallorcans make *butifarras* and I've had them with fennel and also with marjoram, but that's very, very Mallorcan.'

I'm sure you can vary your flavourings to reflect the traditions of Bury, Cork or Paris and I promise I won't set Rachel on you.

Morcilla is often made in smaller-gauge skins and twisted to form small, almost spherical puddings which are fried whole after poaching. If you fancy this. Reduce the poaching time accordingly. I'd suggest 45 minutes as a starting point.

Pâtés and terrines (page 114)

Pâté came from two sources when I was a kid. There was the stuff from the grocery store or the deli that came in oval ceramic crocks (my mother, as I remember, would flirt openly with the spud-faced geriatric in the butchery section, who dispensed the empties as gifts to his 'special ladies'). The tops were ferociously aspicked and coded with various arcane trimmings. The wrinkled orange slice meant the 'Ardennes', a liverish concoction that looked like a lateral section through a life-threatening tumour and may, or may not, have contained duck. Best, though, by far, was *pâté de campagne* (country pâté), which looked like dog food but was packed with enough French military-grade garlic to knock out a passing camel.

Some women in the 1970s were different. They wore huge broad floppy-brimmed hats, had hair like in the ads, ran through fields in soft focus and did all their own cooking. I think Mum was one of those... or at least she thought she was, and so, one dark day, she got a shiny cookbook down from the shelf, bought a pail of guts from the spud-faced butcher and boldly made her own.

I was truly impressed. It was a hell of an achievement and what was more, it made the store-bought stuff taste like year-old meatloaf. I'd never been to France, but now I knew exactly what it would taste like and I was sold on pâté.

A decent pâté de campagne is a thing of beauty and not remotely difficult to knock up. Recipes are legion and variations huge, but that's half the fun. The main points to remember as you go off-piste are that all the flavour is in the marinade and the texture depends on proper cooling while tightly wrapped, so the longer you take over things the more brilliant the finished product will be.

There's something lovely about an even-tempered terrine, and a chicken liver parfait will always be a welcome addition to the starters section, but let's act before it's too late, to rescue the pâté our parents found so exotic.

Confit and rillettes (pages 118 and 121)

There is a whole category of preservation called 'confiting' that involves long, slow poaching in fats or oils. Both pork and duck respond well to this treatment producing deliciously rich rillettes of shredded meat or confit duck legs, the great bistro stand-by. In both cases, the cooked meat is allowed to cool in the fat in which it has cooked and where, deprived of air, it can age and develop flavours safely.

Pork pie (page 124)

These days we expect the crust of a pork pie to be every bit as delicious as the filling but this wasn't always so. The pork pie is a direct descendant of medieval recipes wherein meat was stewed inside an impenetrable casing of flour and fat – it was even called a '**coffyn**'. At the top table, the servants would prise off the lid of the thing to release 4 and 20 blackbirds, or the smell of a rich meat filling, then later, their masters sated, the servants could descend upon the remains – including the 'crust'– to feed themselves.

A pork pie, ever since, has been made of a 'hot water pastry', a simple combination of flour, lard – which is solid at room temperature – and enough hot water to make it malleable. Hot water crust was traditionally stretched upwards or 'raised' around a mould. This was usually a greased wooden plug called a pie dolly. Once the shape had been made, it was allowed to cool and set before the plug was lifted out and replaced with the filling. The crust stayed in shape as it cooked, perhaps sagging a little, but keeping all the goodness inside. The flour in a hot water crust is effectively fried in the fat – and I mean that in a good way.

Unlike rough puff or short pastry used in modern pies and tarts, there is no aim for 'lightness' in a hot water crust. It is substantial, full of weight, strength and structural integrity and is, therefore wholly delicious.

Like a terrine, the solid filling in a pork pie will shrink away from its container as it cooks, creating the void into which pork butchers pour the blessed unction that is pork trotter jelly.

There are people who don't like the jelly in a pork pie and leave it on the side of their plate. These people are wrong and cannot be our friends.

Recipes:
Curing & salting

Basic dry cure

500g/1⅛lb salt
300g/10½oz granulated sugar
2.5g/½ tsp Prague Powder #1 per kg/2¼lb of meat to be cured [1]

Mix the ingredients together in a non-metallic container. Older recipes recommend saltpetre. This contains sodium nitrate, which partially converts to nitrite during curing. It has been used for centuries, but the actual quantities of nitrite that eventually remain in your meat are less easy to control with saltpetre.

Rub vigorously into the surface of the meat. If this doesn't sound too grim, imagine that you're exfoliating. The rough crystals will disrupt the surface cells of the meat and speed up penetration.

Make a bed of the cure in the bottom of your container and lay your massaged meat on top. (On the farm, dry-curing would have taken place in wood or stone troughs or sometimes barrels, and the liquid leached from the meat would be able to run out on to the curing house floor. That will be a bit messy in a modern kitchen, so see page 39 for an alternative dry-curing box.)

Heap the remaining cure on top.

Your cured meat will be ready in about 3 weeks, when it's lost 30% of its starting weight.

---

[1] Available from the supplier listed on page 142. Prague Powder is a mixture of 6.5% sodium nitrite in common salt. The nitrite itself is toxic in large quantities but the Prague Powder is easier to keep, to measure and to use safely. You can obviously leave this out entirely if you wish. The Prague Powder you buy will come with full instructions. If the manufacturers' recommendations vary from mine, please follow theirs.

Basic wet cure

500g/1⅛lb salt
300g/10½oz granulated sugar
2.5g/½ tsp Prague Powder #1 per kg/2¼lb of meat to be cured
(see note on page 70)

Dissolve the ingredients completely in a pan of boiling water.

Remove the brine from the heat and while it's cooling you can add any flavouring ingredients you like – bay leaf, peppercorns, crushed juniper berries would all be traditional – tied up in a piece of clean muslin (cheesecloth).

Once the brine is cool pour it over the meat, in a non-reactive container and then store it in a cool dark place.

It's easy to create a brining set-up small enough to go into your fridge, and modern butchers might well keep big brine barrels in their walk-in fridges, but traditionally a cool pantry or cellar would have been fine, particularly in the cooler months. If you're wet-brining for a long time, it's worth draining off the brine once a week, bringing it up to a rolling boil to kill anything unpleasant, then allowing it to cool before pouring back over.

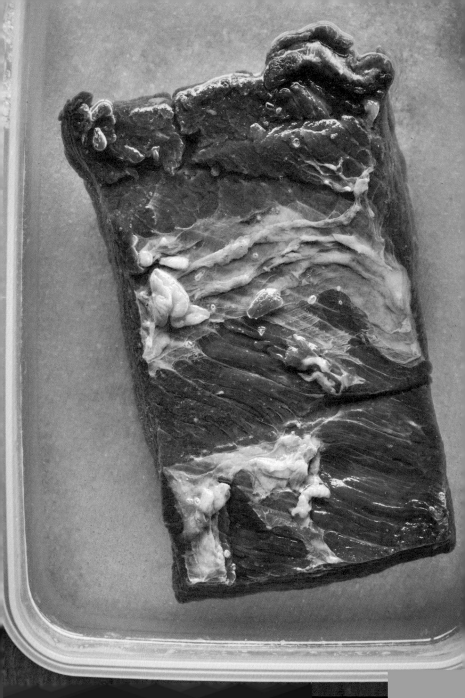

The easy cure

500g/1⅛lb salt
300g/10½oz granulated sugar
2.5g/½ tsp Prague Powder #1 per kg/2¼lb of meat to be cured
   (see note on page 70)

Get hold of a nice fatty piece of belly pork – any size you fancy as long as you can find a zip-seal freezer bag that it will fit into.

Mix all the cure ingredients together in a non-metallic container. Rub a good amount of the dry cure hard into the meat, then put the meat into the bag and pour in the rest of the cure.

Zip it up and put it into the fridge.

Turn it over every day and, after a week, rinse the cure off and pat the meat dry.

Lardo

1 large piece of fat from the back of the pig's neck;
*   it needs to be a good 2.5cm/1 inch thick*
500g/1⅛lb salt
fresh thyme
3 juniper berries, crushed

Trim the fat of any shreds of meat and pare away the skin.

Lay two or three disposable wooden chopsticks in the bottom of a non-reactive dish, then bury them in a layer of salt seasoned with the thyme and juniper berries.

Lay the fat on top of the salt layer and cover it thickly with more of the seasoned salt. The fat will not yield quantities of liquid like meat, so, the chopsticks are usually sufficient to keep the meat in contact with the dry salt and raised out of any pooling moisture.

Cover with plastic wrap and leave in the fridge, turning, pouring off the liquid and re-burying every couple of days. After 10–14 days the lardo should be ready to eat – slice it very thinly while still at fridge temperature, then eat it draped on grilled (broiled) bread on which you've rubbed a cut clove of garlic – but the Italians leave it much longer. Cured backfat has an excellent shelf life, much extended by modern refrigeration, but I've never managed to keep a piece in my fridge for more than a fortnight without eating the lot.

Guanciale

2 pig's cheeks
500g/1⅛lb coarse sea salt
500g/1⅛lb granulated sugar
3 sprigs fresh thyme
15g/½oz black peppercorns

Trim the pig's cheeks carefully. You're looking to create a neat shape and to remove any odd-looking bits. Ragged edges are a temptation to bacteria, and glands and bits of blood vessel are just unappetizing.

Mix the salt, sugar and thyme leaves in a bowl and add the peppercorns, roughly crushed with the back of a spoon.

Rub a good amount of the dry cure into the cheeks as hard as you can. It feels like an expensive exfoliation regime for a reason – you're making sure the cure can penetrate. Heap the cure over the cheeks and leave them, uncovered, in a non-metallic container in the fridge for 5–7 days.

Find a dry, airy spot where you can be sure the temperature won't rise above 16°C (61°F) – a garden shed or cellar works well in the winter months – and hang the cheeks on strings to dry for 3 weeks.

When you're ready to eat, cut them down, scrape off the salt coat and enjoy. Guanciale can be used in the same way as bacon, but is shown off to its best advantage in a rich carbonara or a simple amatriciana.

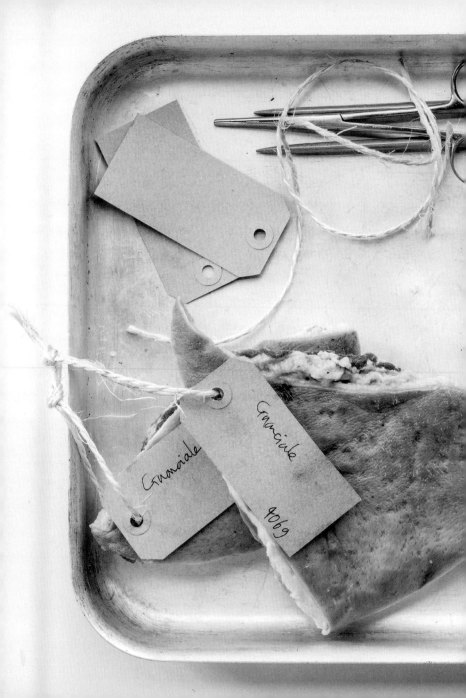

Brining brisket

1.5kg/3⅓lb beef brisket

For the brine:
2kg/4½lb water
200g/7oz salt
75g/2¾oz granulated sugar
15g/½oz Prague Powder #1 (optional), see note on page 70
2 bay leaves
2 cloves garlic
15g/½oz pickling spice (I use a mixture of mace, allspice, juniper,
    coriander, ginger, dried chillies and just a couple of cloves,
    but you can go wherever you fancy with this)

This brined brisket can be used for pastrami and salt beef. The cure for pastrami (see page 83) is traditionally just slightly sweeter, so add 50g/1¾oz of honey if necessary.

Bring all the brine ingredients to the boil and allow to cool.

Pack the brisket into doubled, zip-seal freezer bags.

Ladle in the brine, exclude as much air as you can, then seal both bags.

Place in the fridge and turn daily.

See pages 83 and 84 for timings and method for pastrami and salt beef.

Pastrami

1 quantity brined brisket (see page 80)
10g/¼oz each black peppercorns and coriander seeds

After 5 days in the brine, remove the brisket and pat it dry with paper towel.

Crush the peppercorns and coriander seeds roughly.

Massage hard into the surface of the brisket, trying to get as much to adhere as possible.

Hot-smoke to an internal temperature of 70°C (158°F). You can do this in any covered barbecue. Try to keep the temperature low and steady so the cooking takes as long as possible, and keep chucking handfuls of wood or woodchips on to the fire to keep it good and smoky.

Put your smoked brisket on a rack over a baking pan containing a few centimetres/a couple of inches of boiling water, then build a foil tent around it and seal it up. Try to keep as much free space around the meat as possible, for the steam to circulate.

Put it into the oven at 120°C (250°F) and give it at least 3 hours. A fork should slide into it like butter.

Slice thinly while still hot. Serve hot, in epic quantities on rye bread. You won't need butter, and mayonnaise would be a dangerous error. The pickle is a legal requirement.

Salt beef

1 quantity brined brisket (see page 80)
1 large carrot
1 large white onion
1 bay leaf

Brisket for salt beef can stay in the brine for at least 10 days before being removed, rinsed and patted dry.

Put into a lidded pot, cover with water and add your favourite aromatics. I like to keep things simple with carrots, onions and a bay leaf. You can, if you wish, add more of your pickling spice but I'm not sure it adds anything.

Simmer on top of the stove for between 2 and 4 hours. Keep the water topped up so the meat is covered. It will be done when a skewer runs through it with alarmingly little resistance.

Carve brutally into inelegant slabs while still hot. You can serve the salt beef on a plate with some simply boiled potatoes and some of the veg from the boiling process. Don't, whatever you do, serve the original ones – dredge them out with a ladle and replace with fresh carrots and onions around 20 minutes before serving time. That way you'll have something that tastes authentic but offers at least the possibility of not collapsing into a slurry on the plate.[1] Alternatively, you can use your hot salt beef to build a Reuben (see page 86).

---

[1] There's a terrific and rather forgotten condiment in Ashkenazi Jewish cuisine called *chrain* that goes extremely well with salt beef. To make a quick version, finely grate a couple of cooked beetroot (beets) and add to an equal quantity of bought horseradish sauce. Good chrain has a sweet edge that balances the horseradish, so if your beets aren't sweet enough, add a little granulated sugar.

Proper corned beef

Oh dear. We really are two great nations separated only by a shared language. In the US they make a truly lovely salted beef which Americans call 'corned beef'. This is deeply confusing to us Brits because the 'corned beef' of our childhoods was a canned product – chips of dried, salted beef set in its own fat. In the years before refrigeration, settlers discovered it was possible to breed excellent cattle at minimal cost on the vast Argentine Pampas, but couldn't ship the meat back to Europe without a method of preservation.

Dried and salted beef were both successfully exported, but the most popular product was corned beef, most of which was produced in and exported from the small Uruguayan port town of Fray Bentos.

With the advent of efficient canning, corned beef became the best preserved product with which to sustain soldiers, sailors and explorers on long expeditions. French soldiers in the Napoleonic wars are thought to have given it the grand title of *boeuf boillu* (boiled beef), which the Brits naturally corrupted into 'bully beef'.

In the unlikely event that you have any salt beef left over, chill it and then slice it extremely thinly across the grain of the meat. Having been cooked to rags, it will be simple to break the slices down between your fingers into short shreds which can be bound with melted butter and set into a terrine: an elegant and infinitely more tasty 'homage' to bully beef.

Building a Reuben

Smear two slices of rye bread with a thick layer of thousand island dressing. On one slice, mound a pile of salt beef.

Stack a layer of sauerkraut on top of the meat, then get three or more slices of Emmenthal to sit on its chest and hold it down while you slide the lot under a hot grill (broiler).

Reunite the sandwich with its besmeared lid and serve forth with the statutory pickle. Do not expect to finish the sandwich in a single sitting. That is NOT the point.

Duck 'ham'

10g/¼oz fresh or dried thyme, rosemary or juniper
5g/1 tsp cracked black peppercorns
200g/7oz coarse sea salt
1 duck breast
freshly ground black pepper
butcher's string

Mix the aromatic component with the peppercorns and salt to create a cure. Coat the duck breast with a thick layer, then place in a zip-seal freezer bag or a non-reactive dish and cover with any remaining cure. Refrigerate for 24 hours.

Wash off the cure. Pat the breast dry, season it with a little ground pepper and wrap it in muslin (cheesecloth).

Tie the breast tightly with butcher's string in several places. This holds the breast in a pleasant shape and allows you to hang it without penetrating the meat with a hook.

Hang in a cool airy place (see page 27) for a week.

Slice and serve.

Rabbit loin can be cured in exactly the same way, though it will lose weight quicker as it doesn't have the same flavourful layer of fat and skin.

Recipes:
Drying

Bresaola

single muscle from beef 'top round'
   (usually around 500g–1kg/1⅛lb–2¼lb)
125g/4½oz red wine
100g/3½oz coarse sea salt
100g/3½oz granulated sugar
20g/¾oz fresh or dried rosemary
5g/1 tsp black peppercorns
2.5g/½ tsp Prague Powder #2 per kg/2¼lb of meat
   (see note on page 70)
butcher's string

Ask your butcher for the main muscle in the top round. This is from the top
of the leg, usually regarded as a second-class roast but excellently lean and
close-textured for our purposes. Trim off all the surface fat and silverskin.
Be merciless; it all makes for great stock. Don't, however, try to remove
the single vein of silverskin running through the centre of the muscle
– your meat will fall apart if you do.

Put the meat into a bowl, pour over the red wine and leave to marinate in
the fridge overnight.

Make up your cure by putting the dry ingredients through a grinder, then
put half the cure into an airtight jar and set aside.

Take the meat out of the wine marinade, dry it with paper towel, then rub
the other half of the cure into the surface and seal it in a zip-seal freezer
bag. Place in the fridge and allow to marinate, turning daily. After a week,
take the meat out of the bag, dry it with paper towel again, then rub with
the second half of the cure. Reseal and marinate for a second week.

cont.

Remove any remaining cure from the meat and pat dry with paper towels. Tie two pieces of string vertically around the meat, then tie a series of butcher's knots horizontally around and wrap it in clean muslin (cheesecloth), see illustration opposite.

Label clearly with date and weight and hang in a cool place, not too dry (see page 27). Check regularly by sniffing for unpleasantnesses and weighing carefully. Your bresaola will be ready after around 3 weeks, or when it's lost 30% of its weight. I usually remove the muslin for the last week.

Slice the bresaola paper thin and serve either as it comes or with olive oil and lemon.

The butcher's knot

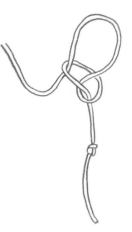

Tie a figure-of-eight knot near the end of your string, leave maybe a 10cm tail

Make a simple slip-knot a little further down the string (note: the top-left end of the string remains attached to the reel)

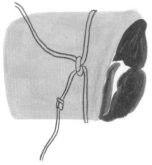
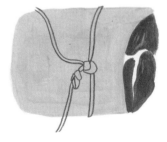

Put the loop of the slip-knot around the meat and pull tight

As you pull on the top string everything slips until the first knot 'locks' the slip-knot. Then cut the string leading to the reel and knot the cut ends together for safety

Salami

1kg/2¼lb pork shoulder
200g/7oz pork backfat
30g/1oz salt
2.5g/½ tsp Prague Powder #2 per kg/2¼lb of meat
  (see note on page 70)
1 clove garlic
2.5g/½ tsp fennel seeds
2.5g/½ tsp cracked black peppercorns
sausage casings
butcher's string

Half an hour in the freezer will make the meat easier to handle.

Remove bones, skin and any stringy connective tissue from the shoulder and slice the meat around 1cm/½ inch thick. Cut each slice into batons, then across into dice.

Go over the pile roughly with a big chopping knife so that part of the meat is more finely and irregularly cut. Skip this phase if you like your salami chunky, spend ages on it if you like it smoother.

Cut the backfat into 1cm/½ inch dice.

Combine the chopped shoulder meat (should be around 800g/1¾lb) with the cubed fat (200g/7oz) and weigh accurately. The proportion for curing is at least 30g/1oz of salt for every kg/2¼lb of meat. Add your Prague Powder #2 to the salt first and mix it thoroughly.

cont.

Select your flavourings. You can go all manner of wild here, but I've stayed basic: one clove of garlic and 2.5g/½ teaspoon each of fennel and black pepper. Grind the flavourings with a pestle and mortar, mix them with your measured salt, then work it all into the meat mixture with your hands. You can also try paprika, rosemary, orange peel or pretty much anything else you fancy. If you're feeling particularly French you can add 150g/5½oz of rough red wine.

Chill the stuffing mix for a couple of hours while soaking the casings (see page 43), then stuff away. Twist and cut your salamis to length, then tie off the ends of the casings in a knot and secure with string. Make a loop at one end.

Examine the salamis carefully and use a needle to pierce the skin and relieve any air bubbles. As the skins dry and tighten they'll tend to drive out excess air, but it will need an exit point.

Weigh each salami and label it with ingredients, date and weight. Calculate what your target weight will be – starting weight minus 30% from moisture loss – and write this on the label too.

Hang your salamis inside for a couple of days while the skins tighten and become papery. Then move them outside to dry. Choose a place where they're under some cover, in clear circulating air and protected from animals and birds. If you have an outdoor shed or garage it might do, or you can rig up a simple hanging cage (see page 37). A dry white mould is acceptable on the outside of the skin, but patches of fur or coloured mould should be washed off as they develop with a weak solution of vinegar in water.

Your salamis will be ready to eat after a month of hanging. You'll know they're done when they have lost around 30% of their weight. They will be softer in texture than many cheap store-bought salamis (which have often been quite literally hanging about for years) and infinitely more delicious.

Jerky

1kg/2¼lb sirloin, silverside or top round of beef
100g/3½oz salt
100g/3½oz Worcestershire, soy or teriyaki sauce
100g/3½oz bourbon, tequila or beer
30g/1oz dried herbs – including thyme, sage and oregano
20g/¾oz mixed chilli powder, onion powder and garlic powder
30g/1oz black peppercorns, roughly cracked
plus/or your own mystery ingredient?

Cut the meat into strips along the grain of the muscle and put them into a non-reactive dish.

Salt the meat for a couple of hours to draw out the moisture.

Combine the ingredients for your wet marinade – that's your liquids plus the herbs and powder mix – and soak the strips in it overnight.

Dry the strips carefully with paper towel and roll them in any dry ingredients that you'd like to form a crust – I particularly like roughly cracked black peppercorns.

Lay or hang the strips in your desiccator, slow oven or jerky box (see page 39).

The jerky will be done when it's still soft enough to tear at manfully with your teeth but before it's hard enough to snap, which, depending on your drying conditions, may take either a few days or a couple of weeks.

Biltong

1kg/2¼lb beef sirloin, silverside or top round
100g/3½oz salt
100g/3½oz cider vinegar
100g/3½oz black peppercorns
100g/3½oz coriander seeds

Slice the meat along the grain into 1cm/½ inch thick strips.

Lay the meat strips in a non-reactive dish, strew with the salt and mix thoroughly with your hands to ensure good coverage. Store covered in the fridge for 2 hours.

Pat the meat dry with paper towels, carefully removing any remaining salt. Paint the meat with the vinegar, using a pastry brush.

Crush the peppercorns and coriander seeds or blitz them momentarily in a grinder, then lay the vinegar-coated meat on them and press down so the ingredients adhere.

You can arrange the strips on the grating of your desiccator or an oven cooling rack or hang them in your biltong box (see page 39).

The biltong is done when it's almost black on the outside and has a tight, rubbery consistency inside. In the biltong box, and if the meat is cut thin, this can be as short as a couple of days. It will keep in the fridge in an airtight box for up to 2 months, and much longer if frozen in small batches.

Lomo

200g/7oz salt
20g/¾oz pimentón (smoked paprika – the hot type), plus extra
  for coating
100g/3½oz granulated sugar
1 whole pork loin (tenderloin and silverskin removed)
butcher's string

Mix the salt, sugar and pimentón to form the cure.

Put the cure into a bag or a non-reactive dish and pack in the trimmed pork loin. Put it into the fridge. I usually salt a 1kg/2¼lb loin for 3 days, but vary this time depending on the weight and thickness of your loin.

Rinse off the cure, pat the loin dry, then powder it lightly with more of the smoked paprika.

Wrap the loin in muslin (cheesecloth) and tie a series of butcher's knots along its length (see page 95).

Weigh the loin and mark the weight and date on a label before hanging.

Hang in a cool, airy place (see page 27) until 30% weight loss is achieved.

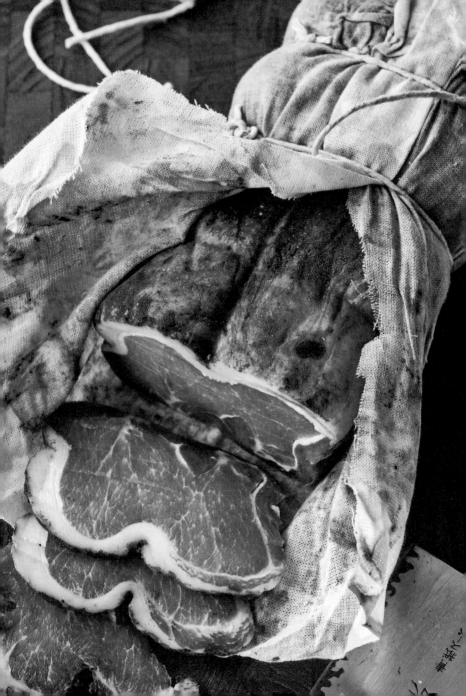

Recipes: More good things

Classic sausages

natural sausage casings (see page 142 for suppliers)
5g/1 tsp dried savory
2.5g/½ tsp dried sage
2.5g/½ tsp allspice berries
2.5g/½ tsp white peppercorns
1kg/2¼lb pork back
1kg/2¼lb pork belly
15g/½oz salt
200g/7oz white breadcrumbs, dried in the oven

Soak the casings in several changes of clean water to remove the salt.

Select your spicing mix. For a traditional English breakfast-style sausage I suggest savory, sage, allspice and white peppercorns in the amounts above. You'll also need plenty of salt. Grind the spice mix in a pestle and mortar, but keep the salt to one side.

Remove any skin and bones from the pork and slice the meat into cubes small enough to fit into the throat of your mincer (meat grinder). Salt generously, then put into a freezer for half an hour or so. This stiffens the meat and makes mincing easier.

Pass the meat through the mincer once. I prefer a coarse plate for a chunkier sausage, but use a fine one or pass the meat through twice if you want something more smooth and store-bought in style.

cont.

Add the breadcrumbs (10% by weight) and half your spice mix and work thoroughly through the meat with your hands. Fry a teaspoonful in a hot pan (skillet) to check the seasoning and adjust accordingly, using the other half of the spice mix. The breadcrumbs soak up some of the fat and juices that might otherwise be cooked out of the sausage, so drying them carefully in the oven before adding them to the mix will ensure that they are super-absorbent.

Slip the wet casing over the funnel attachment of your mincer.

Remove the blades from the mincer, mount the stuffing funnel and set the machine going on its slowest setting. Keep your fingers around the rolled casing, paying it out as required. Leave a good length of casing empty before starting to fill.

Don't allow the meat to pack too tight, but try to avoid allowing air in either. Beginners should fill about a metre/40 inches of casing at a time then cut it off, leaving plenty of spare casing at either end.

Tie off one end of each length of casing, then gently squeeze enough space to twist the sausage a few times between each link.

Cooking a proper sausage

…and by that I mean one with a **high meat content**, well-packed in a natural casing, is a matter of delicately balancing heat so the meat cooks without the pressure of the expanding filling bursting the skin.[1] Some people – I name no names – seem to enjoy pricking the sausage, believing that the relief of pressure will prevent the banger bursting. This will, of course, stop the skin splitting uncontrollably but only at terrible cost: allowing all the juices to escape into the pan.

Sausage prickers convince themselves that the leaked liquid is largely fat and thus conclude that a pierced sausage is a healthier sausage. Further still, to entirely rob it of its vital fluids and turn it into a health food, they like to grill (broil) or roast it in a hot oven – because frying means fat and fat is evil. Oh yes, the stabbed and grilled sausage is a healthy, sensible and nourishing foodstuff; it's also a shrivelled, limp travesty and an insult to the proud majesty of the banger.

There is, to my mind, only one way to correctly cook a proper sausage. Take a deep-sided frying pan (skillet) and pour in enough oil to come halfway up the sides. Slip in the sausages, bring the oily bath up to a temperature at which they barely simmer and hold them there. The intention is not to shallow-fry the sausage but to lovingly poach it. The skin, remember, is impermeable to fat, so none is going to leak in or out. The oil bath anoints the casing, keeping it supple so it is less inclined to split and the gentle cooking preserves all the juices inside the banger. This is not a speedy, slapdash process – at least half an hour is required for the full ritual – but at the end the sausage is firm, bursting with rich juices, lightly tanned and requiring only a brief wipe with a cloth before being proudly served.

[1] … in case you were wondering why we Brits call it a 'banger'.

Failing this, massage each sausage individually with oil first, then slide them into an oiled pan and keep them rolling, on a low heat, for as long and as continuously as possible.

Trust me, even 25 minutes of gently rolling them back and forth, jostling their plumply greased little bodies against each other, is not too long. As the skins change to a light tan, then begin to caramelize as the **Maillard reaction** takes place, you'll find yourself shifting into the right meditative state to honour your sausage.

Sausage variations

Sausage recipes can be varied in all sorts of directions from the basic recipe:

- Vary the herbs. Sage is traditional with pork in the UK, juniper works brilliantly with game, and more Mediterranean oily herbs like thyme or oregano combine well with garlic. Quantities are entirely a matter of taste, but if you start with small pinches, testing samples in the frying pan (skillet) as you go, you'll build flavours quickly without endangering the whole batch.

- If you want to add a fruit element in the form of prune, apricot or apple, use 20g/¾oz dried fruit per kg/2¼lb of sausage meat, chop it finely and work it through the mixture.

- A Cumberland sausage is simply seasoned, predominantly with pepper, and formed into a coil without twisting into individual links. Hold it together in a spiral shape with wooden skewers for cooking.

- Use a splash of red wine, chopped smoked bacon and a healthy amount of crushed garlic – say 10g/¼oz per kg/2¼lb – in your sausage meat for a reasonably authentic *saucisson de Toulouse*. This is the sausage to use in a cassoulet.

- Adding 10g/¼oz of smoked paprika per kg/2¼lb and cutting the pork fat into coarser cubes gives a good chorizo.

- Adding fennel (5g/1 teaspoon) and minced garlic (10g/¼oz) to the mix makes very acceptable Italian *salsicce*.

- Try replacing the lean back pork with beef, lamb or venison, but always retain the fatty pork, which is still necessary for texture.

- By replacing the pork entirely with equal quantities of lamb shoulder and lamb breast and seasoning liberally with harissa paste, you'll end up with enviable merguez.

The world isn't just your oyster, it's also your sausage.

Pâté de campagne

500g/1⅛lb pork shoulder
250g/9oz pig's liver
250g/9oz pork backfat
2 rashers (slices) unsmoked back bacon
caul fat or 10 rashers streaky bacon
1 egg
salt

For the marinade:
5g/1 tsp chopped fresh parsley
2 sprigs fresh thyme
3 allspice berries
75g/2¾oz sherry
75g/2¾oz white wine
black pepper

Cut all the meaty ingredients, except for the caul fat or streaky bacon, into rough 2cm/¾ inch cubes.

Chop the herbs finely, crush the berries, then mix all the marinade ingredients together with the meat in a plastic bag with lots of black pepper. Leave in the fridge for at least 24 hours.

Discard the marinade, then mince (grind) the meat coarsely or blitz lightly in a food processor. Don't purée unless you like it boringly smooth (this is *pâté de campagne*, not *pâté de suburb*).

cont.

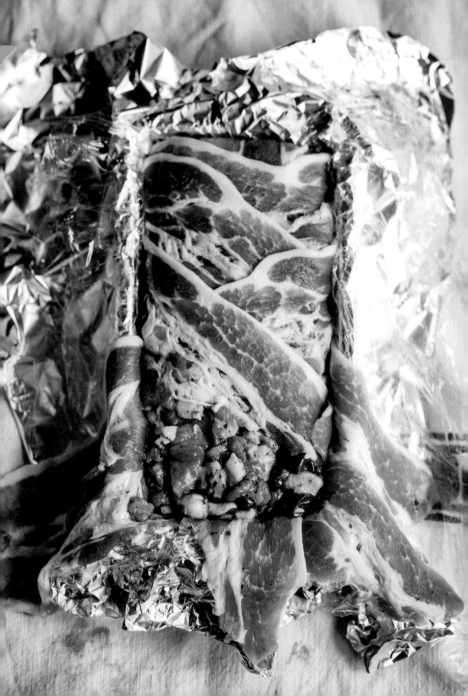

Prepare your tin. A terrine tin with a lid is great, but you can use a regular loaf tin with sloping sides. If you are a perfectionist, you can cut a lid from a piece of wood or thick card and wrap it in foil. Line your tin with a layer of foil, a layer of plastic wrap and a single layer of caul fat. Try to keep the fat evenly spread out – it's mainly a decorative wrapping. If you can't get caul fat you can line the tin with bacon rashers (bacon is never inappropriate).

Add the egg and 15g/½oz of salt to the mixture and work through with your hands. Pack the mixture into the prepared tin, folding the caul fat closed over the top.

Preheat the oven to 180°C (350°F). Wrap the plastic wrap around to form a tight seal, then close up the foil before putting on your lid or your foil-covered board (the lid isn't vital but makes for a more elegant finished product). Place the tin in a big roasting pan and pour in boiling water to just below the top of the tin. Slide it carefully into the oven and allow to cook gently for 2½ hours.

Remove the terrine from the oven and weight the lid. Do not be tempted to unwrap at this stage. Once it's cool enough, transfer to the fridge overnight, keeping the weights in place.

Unwrap, like a large and meaty pass-the-parcel. While cooling, the pâté will have reabsorbed most of its juices and fats, which will then have set. Wipe the surface clean of excess jelly and fat to expose that lovely layer of caul. If you're feeling rustic, you can smear the jelly on your bread before serving.

Duck confit

30g/1oz salt
15g/½oz black peppercorns, crushed
4 sprigs fresh thyme
4 cloves garlic, crushed
4 large duck legs
750g/1lb ⅝oz duck fat, melted

Mix the salt, crushed peppercorns, thyme leaves and crushed garlic in a bowl and rub the mixture hard into all surfaces and crevices of the duck legs.

Allow the duck legs to cure overnight in the fridge, then rinse off the marinade and pat the legs dry with paper towel.

Pack the duck legs skin side down into a pot, casserole or roasting pan so that they cover the bottom neatly in a single layer. Pour over the melted fat to cover the meat, and poach gently at 85–90°C (185–203°F) for 3 hours.

To store the confit, pack the cooled legs into a jar, pot or plastic box and pour over enough of the fat to cover. Tap smartly on the worktop to dislodge any air bubbles before allowing to cool and set. Store the confit in the fridge. Each time you remove a leg to use, gently re-melt the fat so it settles back neatly, sealing the remaining confit.

To serve a duck leg, drop it skin side down into a hot, dry pan. This will crisp and brown the skin beautifully. Then flip it over to quickly sear the other side. Remember you're not cooking the duck here, just warming it through while making the exterior doubly delicious. Serve with potatoes, roasted or fried in some of the fat from the same jar, and a green salad or green beans.

cont.

As you work your way down through the confit you'll find you have more fat left over than you strictly need, so hoick out a lump every now and again to fry potatoes or even (be still, my bleating heart surgeon) your breakfast eggs.

This recipe will also work well for goose, which like duck has a delicate flavour that's present in the abundant fat. It doesn't work so well for chicken, which somehow just comes out bland when confited. The tough legs of any of the small game birds can be confited and are often served as such alongside the breast fillets, which have been more speedily cooked. As they lack fat of their own, they are usually done in duck fat.

Rabbit and pork rillettes

1 rabbit
500g/1⅛lb fat belly pork, skin removed
10g/¼oz salt
15 ground black peppercorns
10 sprigs fresh thyme, chopped
4 sprigs fresh rosemary, chopped
3 bay leaves
10 cloves garlic, chopped
16 juniper berries
30g/1oz olive oil

Skin the rabbit and joint it into pieces – or have your butcher do it for you.
Cut the pork into chunky cubes. Put the meat into a dish.

Combine the salt, ground peppercorns, half the fresh thyme and rosemary,
the 3 bay leaves and half the garlic and rub into the rabbit pieces. Cover
and allow to marinate overnight in the fridge.

Preheat the oven to 120°C (250°F). Pack the rabbit, pork pieces and
marinade into a casserole or other heavy, lidded pot, sprinkling the
remaining seasonings between the pieces. Pour over the olive oil.

Cut a circle of greaseproof paper big enough to sit on the surface of the
oil and make a small hole in the centre to act as a steam vent. Lay on
the paper cover, then put the lid on and place the casserole in the oven
for 3 hours. Check occasionally. As the pork renders down, there should
be enough fat to cover everything. If not, top up with extra olive oil. The
fat should not simmer, maybe just the occasional bubble, and a probe

cont.

thermometer should read between 100–120°C (200–250°F). Shift the meat pieces every now and then, just to make sure they're not sticking.

When the meat is soft, allow it to cool in the fat a little, then pour through a sieve and collect all the melted fat

Carefully pick off all the rabbit meat with your fingers and, along with the pork, shred it as fine as you like into a bowl.

Pour some of the warm fat back over the meat, stirring until it comes together into a mass. Taste and adjust the seasoning.

Pack the rillettes into jars or pots and top with more fat, knocking the container on a countertop to dislodge any air bubbles.

Refrigerate. Rillettes will last up to a week in the fridge and can be frozen for much longer. Allow to return to room temperature before serving with sourdough, preferably toasted.

Pork pie

For the filling:
1kg/2¼lb boned pork shoulder, skin on
200g/7oz commercial unsmoked bacon
2.5g/½ tsp each ground mace, nutmeg, allspice and black
    peppercorns
2.5g/½ tsp chopped fresh sage leaves
10g/¼oz salt
1 quantity hot water crust pastry (see page 131)
1 egg, for eggwash

For the jelly:
1 split pig's trotter
1 stick celery
1 carrot
2 bay leaves
2–3 fresh sage leaves

Trim the skin and tough connective tissue from the boned pork shoulder
and save it. These will be vital elements of the jelly later. Cut the meat into
rough 1cm/½ inch dice.

Cut the bacon into similar-sized pieces. In commercially produced pies,
nitrites are added to keep the filling an appetizing colour. There are enough
residual preservatives in store-bought bacon to keep the pie filling pink
throughout. If this thought worries you, you can leave out the bacon for an
authentically rustic, grey pie interior.

To make the jelly, chuck your porky trimmings into a pot with the split pig's
trotter, celery, carrot, bay leaves and sage. Cover with cold water and

cont.

allow to barely simmer for 2–3 hours, until the trotter gives up the ghost and collapses. Strain the liquid through muslin (cheesecloth) and keep it in the fridge. Check that it sets to a good consistency – if it doesn't, you can reduce it a little further. This will produce much more jelly than you need but it freezes well, and I like to serve it chopped as a side dish with the pie.

Mix the spices with the chopped sage leaves and a good 10g/¼oz of salt and season your meat. Remember that the pie is a preserved product, so this is as much about curing as flavouring.

Mix the meat and seasonings thoroughly by hand and then blitz half the mix in a food processor before recombining. I like chunks of pork in my pies, but you can vary proportions here to suit your own taste.

Preheat the oven to 180°C (350°F). Cut off a quarter of your dough to use for the lid. Roll out the remaining dough, fold, turn and reroll until it begins to feel smooth and elastic. Roll to a large circle to line your pie tin. Mould the pastry to fit the tin and allow an overhang of at least 2cm/¾ inch. You can grease it if you think there's not enough fat in this recipe already, but it's not remotely necessary. My tin is round, 16cm/6¼ inches across, 7cm/2¾ inches deep, with a loose bottom. You shouldn't need a springform, as the pie shrinks away from the sides as it cooks and pops out clean.

Carefully pack your filling into the case, taking care to avoid any air gaps.

Form a lid with the remaining pastry and glue it on with eggwash, then trim the excess and crimp the edges. Make a small hole in the centre of the pie. Finally, eggwash the top, place the pie on a baking sheet and put into the preheated oven. After 90 minutes, carefully remove the pie from the tin, eggwash again and return to the oven for 5–10 more minutes.

Once the pie is cool, wrap the base and sides in plastic wrap. Warm some of the jelly in a pan and pour it slowly through a funnel to fill the air gap between filling and case. Keep tapping the pie gently on the worktop to expel any air bubbles. Put the pie into the fridge so the jelly can set.

Gala pie

I must have first encountered gala pie at a family wedding, funeral or other licensed brawl. It was a symbol of celebration, a sophisticated refinement on the quotidian pub pork pie. While uncles fought and boasted and aunts consoled themselves with gin and recrimination, I sat under a table on beer-soaked carpet and wondered at the infinite egg. How was it possible that every slice of the yard-long, loaf-shaped pie had a pristine slice of egg in it? Was it even a hen that laid it? Perhaps it was laid by a gala… whatever that was. (I think I probably worried too much as a child.)

In my less troubled maturity, I discovered that the infinite egg is a simple trick. A quantity of eggs are separated and the yolks loosely beaten together before being poured into a narrow gauge of sausage skin. After a few minutes in hot water the yolk 'sausage' can be peeled and then carefully inserted into a larger skin along with the combined whites, for a further poaching. Of course, the creation of the authentic unappetizing grey ring around the yolk is, and must ever remain, a trade secret.

These days I love a good pie and, though the process has many steps, they are all simple and almost always guarantee a good result. The gala pie is one of those projects that can happily take up an afternoon, but the effect on the audience of wheeling it out is worth all the effort. Rather than indulging in the admittedly hilarious shenanigans of poaching eggs in sausage skins, this recipe contains a simple trick for presentation using whole eggs. It's also worth noting that some consider a gala pie should also contain chicken. You can, if you wish, introduce a layer of poached or leftover roast chicken above or below the eggs. I personally consider this to be a ridiculous affectation, possibly even French.

cont.

1 quantity pork pie ingredients (both filling and jelly, see page 124)
4 eggs

Now, follow the pork pie method on pages 124–126 until you have mixed the meat and seasonings and then blitzed half the mix before recombining.

Place 4 eggs in a pan of cold water, bring to the boil, simmer for exactly 4 minutes, then plunge them into iced water.

Preheat the oven to 180°C (350°F). Cut off a quarter of your dough to use for the lid. Roll out the remaining dough, fold, turn and reroll until it begins to feel smooth and elastic. Roll to a large circle to line your pie tin. Mould the pastry to fit the tin and allow an overhang of at least 2cm/¾ inch. You can grease it if you think there's not enough fat in this recipe already, but it's not necessary. My tin is round, 16cm/6¼ inches across, 7cm/2¾ inches deep, with a loose bottom. You shouldn't need a springform, as the pie shrinks away from the sides as it cooks and pops out clean.

Put a thin layer of meat into the bottom of the pie case, followed by your peeled eggs. Now here's the cunning bit – make a pen mark on the side of the dish on the centre line of one of your eggs. Carefully pack more filling around and over your eggs, trying to avoid any air gaps.

Attach the lid, trim the excess and crimp the edges. Finally, eggwash the top, place the pie on a baking sheet and put into the preheated oven. After 90 minutes, carefully remove the pie from the tin, eggwash again and return to the oven for 5–10 more minutes.

Once the pie is cool, wrap the base and sides in plastic wrap. Warm some of the jelly in a pan and pour it slowly through a funnel to fill the air gap between filling and case. Keep tapping the pie gently on the worktop to expel any air bubbles. Put the pie into the fridge so the jelly can set.

Slice neatly through the guidelines in the crust and serve.

Hot water crust pastry

500g/1⅛lb strong white bread flour
5g/1 tsp salt
125g/4½oz water
175g/6oz commercial lard or carefully hoarded beef fat

Mix the flour in a bowl with the salt. Bring the water to the boil in a pan and melt the lard or dripping in it, then pour the hot liquid into the bowl of flour and begin combining it with a palette knife.

As soon as the dough is cool enough to handle, work it together with your fingers, then form it into a ball. Leave to cool and rest for a few minutes before using. The dough needs to be warm enough to be workable, but if you don't rest it a little it remains elastic and will contract when baked.

This amount will make about 700g/1½lb of pastry.

Blood sausage

1kg/2¼lb pig's blood (see page 43)
350g/12oz coarsely diced pork backfat
300g/10½oz whole milk
60g/2¼oz oatmeal
15g/½oz salt
3 medium onions
large-gauge sausage casings (see page 43)

Mix the blood with the rest of the ingredients apart from the casings and pour or spoon into the skins. Don't overfill, as the filling will expand as it cooks. Try to leave some slack in the skin before tying off, but also ensure there are no air pockets. A centimetre or so of skin, squeezed flat and empty, before the knot should do the trick.

Gently poach the puddings in water just short of a full simmer for 90 minutes, at the end of which time they should be firm and cooked through. Allow to cool in the poaching liquid.

The puddings should be sliced cold and fried before serving. They can be stored under refrigeration for a day or two but should be vacuum-packed or plastic-wrapped and frozen if you want to store them for longer. If you freeze the pudding in slices you will find they defrost quickly… often in the time it takes to properly fry a sausage (see page 110).

You can serve your black pudding in the classic manner, fried crisp on the outside and surrounded by the supportive elements of a Full English Breakfast. Profoundly unpatriotic as it may seem, I like mine crumbled and fried with equal quantities of cubed chorizo, stirred into lightly scrambled eggs and served rolled in a burrito. To be really elegant, slice thinly and serve fried with slices of a sharp, acidic apple, such as a Cox's Orange Pippin (Early Windsor, Fiesta or Kidd's Orange Red).

A final note

It sometimes feels that every recipe we read is offering a quick and simple 'solution' to our meal problems.

There's a place for this kind of thing in busy lives but there's another side to cooking. If we enjoy making food, we should feel it's OK to relax into it, to take our time.

By their very nature, charcuterie recipes are some of the longest we have. You can't rush the process of preservation; you can expect the results to last, perhaps even quietly maturing and improving, for months.

There are few practices more gentle and contemplative. You don't need to trek up a mountain and meditate on the meaning of life – just slow down, salt, dry and cure.

Index & suppliers

Index

Suppliers

All of these suppliers deliver to Europe and the rest of the world, though some ask you to contact them for availability of products and shipping costs so do check before buying.

NISBETS

nisbets.co.uk
The Nisbets catalogue is a sort of bible in professional kitchens. Pots, pans and general professional equipment. Also a good source for cheap probe thermometers.

FRANCO'S FAMOUS SAUSAGEMAKING

sausagemaking.org
Franco's Famous sausagemaking. org is the go-to site for sausage skins, filling machines, brine pumps, in the smaller quantities you will need. Best supplier for Prague Powders, or, if you're not confident in your measuring, of pre-made brine mixes.

LAKELAND

lakeland.co.uk
Between the odd gadgets there's a matchless range of plastic storage containers, zip-seal freezer bags and vacuum-packing gear.

THERMAPEN

thermapen.co.uk
Once you have the hang of internal temperatures, you'll never want to be without a probe thermometer again and you might want to fork out an extra few quid for a really swish one.

WESCHENFELDER

weschenfelder.co.uk
Weschenfelder is one of the world's foremost professional butchery suppliers. Knives, hooks, twine, saws and sausage stuffers.

Managing Director **Sarah Lavelle**
Commissioning Editor **Stacey Cleworth**
Head of Design **Claire Rochford**
Series Designer **Will Webb**
Designer **Gemma Hayden**
Illustrator **Lucia Vinti**
Photographer **Chris Terry**
Head of Production **Stephen Lang**
Senior Production Controller **Nikolaus Ginelli**

Published in 2022 by Quadrille,
an imprint of Hardie Grant Publishing

Quadrille
52–54 Southwark Street
London SE1 1UN
quadrille.com

Cataloguing in Publication Data: a catalogue record for this book is
available from the British Library.

9781787138155

Printed in China

MIX
Paper from
responsible sources
FSC™ C020056
www.fsc.org

DISCLAIMER: The recipes in this book were developed in metric
quantities. The author strongly suggests that you follow the metric
measurements to achieve the best results.